Get Crafty Outdoors

Science and Craft Projects with

ROCKS
AND SOIL

by Ruth Owen

PowerKiDS press

New York

Published in 2013 by The Rosen Publishing Group, Inc.
29 East 21st Street, New York, NY 10010

Produced for Rosen by Ruby Tuesday Books Ltd
Editor for Ruby Tuesday Books Ltd: Mark J. Sachner
US Editor: Sara Antill
Designer: Emma Randall
Consultant: Suzy Gazlay

Cover, 1, 4–5, 6–7, 8, 10, 11 (top), 11 (bottom), 14, 16–17, 18–19, 22 (top), 23, 26–27 © Shutterstock; 9, 12–13, 20–21, 24–25, 28–29 © Ruby Tuesday Books Ltd; 11 (center) © Simm Sepp, Wikipedia Creative Commons; 15 © Wikipedia Creative Commons; 22 (bottom) © istockphoto.

Publisher Cataloging Data

Owen, Ruth, 1967–
        Science and craft projects with rocks and soil / by Ruth Owen.
p.   cm. — (Get crafty outdoors)
Includes index.
Summary: This book tells about the three different types of rock and how each is formed, and includes instructions for six craft projects.
Contents: Our rocky planet — Making rocks—igneous rocks — Make a rock sculpture — Sediment, sand, and soil — Sand art paperweights — Making rocks—sedimentary rocks — Pebble pictures — Making rocks—metamorphic rocks — Make a rock display case — Minerals, gemstones, and crystals — Make your own crystals — Fossils — Make a fossil.
ISBN 978-1-4777-0246-8 (library binding) — ISBN 978-1-4777-0255-0 (pbk.) — ISBN 978-1-4777-0256-7 (6-pack)
        1. Rocks—Juvenile literature   2. Soils—Juvenile literature   3. Handicraft—Juvenile literature   (1. Rocks   2. Soils   3. Handicraft)   I. Title
                2013
        552—dc23

Manufactured in the United States of America

CPSIA Compliance Information: Batch #W13PK7: For Further Information contact Rosen Publishing, New York, New York at 1-800-237-9932

Contents

Our Rocky Planet 4

Making Rocks—Igneous Rocks................................6

Make a Rock Sculpture 8

Sediment, Sand, and Soil................................... 10

Sand Art Paperweights 12

Making Rocks—Sedimentary Rocks 14

Pebble Pictures... 16

Making Rocks—Metamorphic Rocks 18

Make a Rock Display Case 20

Minerals, Gemstones, and Crystals....................22

Make Your Own Crystals 24

Fossils 26

Make a Fossil 28

Glossary 30

Websites..31

Read More, Index 32

Our Rocky Planet

Earth is a very rocky place. There are huge mountains made from rock. We can pick up pebbles on beaches and dig up stones in gardens. So why is there so much rock nearly everywhere we look?

Our planet is completely covered with a thick layer, or **crust**, of rock. This is why we can see and find lots of rock around us.

When you look at a mountain or the Grand Canyon, you are actually seeing a section of the Earth's rocky crust.

This book is all about the rocks that form the outer layer of our planet. You will find out lots of great rock facts and get the chance to make some cool rock crafts.

The Grand Canyon

rocks on a beach

This piece of rock has precious green emeralds in it.

Rocks Rock!

There are hundreds of different types of rocks. Scientists and rock collectors sort rocks into three main groups called **igneous rocks, sedimentary rocks,** and **metamorphic rocks.**

Making Rocks—
Igneous Rocks

New rocks are forming, or being made, all the time. The way that a rock forms tells us whether it is an igneous, sedimentary, or metamorphic rock.

One way that igneous rocks form is through the eruption of a **volcano**.

Below the Earth's crust, it is so hot that rock melts. It becomes thick, superhot, liquid rock called **magma**.

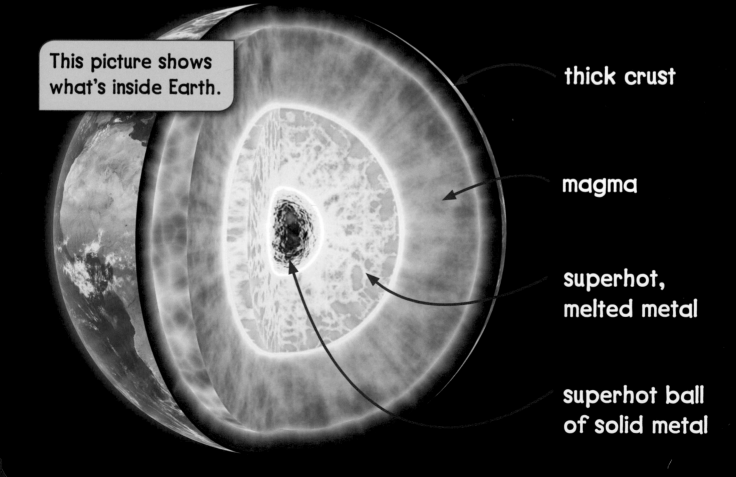

This picture shows what's inside Earth.

thick crust

magma

superhot, melted metal

superhot ball of solid metal

Sometimes, during a volcanic eruption, magma from inside Earth explodes or pours out of a volcano. Once the hot magma is outside of the volcano, it is known as **lava**. As the lava cools, it gets hard and becomes igneous rock.

magma

an erupting
volcano

lava

Rock from Magma

Sometimes igneous rock forms deep underground. Magma oozes up into cracks in the Earth's crust. Then the magma cools down and becomes hard igneous rock.

This obsidian rock is made of lava from a volcano.

This granodiorite rock formed underground from magma.

Make a Rock Sculpture

People have been making **sculptures** from rock for thousands of years. Try collecting rocks and pebbles and make your own rock sculptures for your home or yard.

You will need:

- Pebbles and rocks
- A small brush
- Warm water and soap
- Modeling clay
- Strong glue
- Acrylic paint
- Paintbrushes
- Clear varnish (available online and from craft stores)
- An adult teammate to go pebble hunting with you

Get Crafty:

1 You can find pebbles at the beach or at the edges of a lake or river. Ask friends, neighbors, or family members if you can go pebble hunting in their gardens, too. You can also buy pebbles from garden centers.

2 Look at the shapes of the pebbles you find and be inspired by their shapes to get creative!

3 Use the small brush to scrub the pebbles clean in warm water and soap. Then allow them to dry.

4 If you are making a sculpture with more than one pebble, test out your idea first. Join the pebbles together with little blobs of modeling clay.

5 Glue the pebbles together. Follow the instructions on the glue's packaging. While the glue dries, you can help the pebbles stay in place by wedging modeling clay around them.

modeling clay

6 When the glue is dry, paint your model.

7 Sometimes, the natural colors of pebbles can work really well. The rock dog in the photograph below was made using white stones. The brown spots were then painted on.

natural rock color

Sediment, Sand, and Soil

Sedimentary rocks are made from tiny pieces of rock called sediment. A piece of sediment may only be the size of a grain of sugar. So how does sediment form?

Rock may be hard, but wind and rain can wear it away. As wind blows past a large rock or rainwater washes over it, tiny pieces break off.

On the seashore, waves crash against rock cliffs and break off tiny pieces. All these tiny pieces of rock become sediment.

rock cliff

waves

Sand is a type of sediment. If you look at sand through a magnifying glass, you will see it is made from billions of tiny pieces of rock!

a close-up picture of sand

What Is Dirt Made Of?

Dirt, or soil, in gardens is made from tiny pieces of rock. It looks different than sand because it contains other ingredients. Soil also has tiny pieces of dead plants and animals mixed up with the rock.

Sand Art Paperweights

Try making these cool sand paperweights or ornaments by filling glass jars and bottles with layers of colored sand.

You will need:

- Clear bottles or jars with lids
- Sand from a toy or craft store
- Wax paper
- Cutting board
- Colored chalk
- Small bowls (one for each color of sand)
- A funnel
- Pebbles, shells, beads, or glitter

Get Crafty:

1 Collect clear jars and bottles with lids.

2 Place a sheet of wax paper on a cutting board. Spread out sand over the paper.

3 Now roll a stick of chalk back and forth over the sand. Keep rolling until enough chalk has mixed with the sand to completely color the sand. Tip the sand into a small bowl.

4 Now repeat step 3 with other chalk colors.

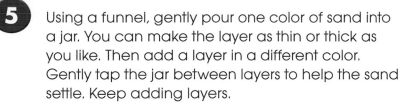

5 Using a funnel, gently pour one color of sand into a jar. You can make the layer as thin or thick as you like. Then add a layer in a different color. Gently tap the jar between layers to help the sand settle. Keep adding layers.

6 You can fill the jar only with sand, or add other decorations, too. Try adding a layer of pretty pebbles. You can also place colorful beads, shells, or glitter in the jar.

7 When the jar is filled, press down on the sand firmly with your fingers. This will press the layers together as much as possible. Then place the lid on tightly.

Making Rocks— Sedimentary Rocks

Sedimentary rock is made from many layers of sediment. When sedimentary rock forms, it's like nature making a giant rock sandwich.

It all begins with a layer of sediment. Then another layer of sediment settles on top. Then another and another. Very slowly, layer after layer builds up.

It's easy to see the different layers in this sandstone sedimentary rock.

All that rock weighs so much that the layers at the bottom are changed by the pressure. The layers of sediment are so tightly pressed together that they actually join together to make solid rock.

This process doesn't happen quickly. It can take millions of years for sedimentary rock to form.

This type of sedimentary rock is called limestone.

Making a Rock Sandwich

Layers of sediment can build up in many ways. For example, rainwater with tiny bits of rock in it might wash into a river. Then the river carries this sediment into a lake. Over millions of years, layers of sediment will build up at the bottom of the lake.

Pebble Pictures

It's possible to make instant works of art with pebbles at the beach or in a garden. You can photograph your artwork and use the images to make greetings cards.

You will need:

- Pebbles
- A bucket
- A flat surface, such as a beach or garden patio or terrace
- A digital camera
- Colorful construction paper or thin cardboard
- Scissors
- Glue
- Color pens
- White printer paper
- A printer and computer, or a photo printer
- An adult to be your teammate and help with cutting, using the camera, and printing the photos

Get Crafty:

 1 First collect lots of pebbles in a bucket. Now it's time to get creative! Arrange the pebbles in your own patterns and designs on the flat surface.

2 When you have finished each picture, ask an adult to help you take a photograph of it.

3 Print out the photographs. You can print them big or small. Then ask an adult to help you cut them out.

4 Make greetings cards by folding pieces of construction paper or thin cardboard in half. Then stick pebble art photographs to the paper or cardboard.

5 You can write personal messages onto your cards, too!

Get Well Soon Grandpa!

To Mom!

Happy Valentine's Day

Making Rocks—
Metamorphic Rocks

Sometimes, one type of rock changes to become a new type of rock.

Rocks can be pressed down under the weight of other rocks. They may also be baked by heat underground. Being heated and pressed together can change an igneous or sedimentary rock into something new—a metamorphic rock.

Sometimes, one type of metamorphic rock can change into a different type of metamorphic rock.

There are so many different types of rock that people collect them. You can start a rock collection by looking in a backyard or at a beach.

These rocks are types of metamorphic rock.

gneiss

quartzite

marble

The outside of the Washington Monument is made from blocks of metamorphic marble rock.

Be a Rock Collector

When you find a new rock, keep a record of where you found it. Then check out your rock.

- How much does it weigh?
- What is its size and shape?
- Is it colorful, dull, or shiny?
- Is it rough or smooth?
- How hard is it? Can you scratch it with your fingernail or a coin?

If you don't know what the rock is, borrow a rock identification book from the library.

Make a Rock Display Case

When you start rock collecting, you will need a place to keep and show off your rocks. You can make this great rock display case from egg cartons and an empty cereal box.

You will need:

- An empty cereal box
- Empty egg cartons
- Scissors
- Tape
- Paint
- Paintbrushes
- Glue
- An adult to help you with cutting

Get Crafty:

1 Cut one side from an empty cereal box. Then trim down the four sides of the box so that it forms a tray about 1 inch (2.5 cm) deep.

2 Stick the corners of the tray together with tape. Stick the tape inside the tray so it doesn't show.

lid

3 Cut the lids and front flaps off the egg cartons.

front flap

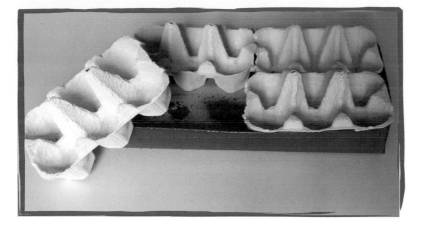

 4 Now you need to fill the tray with egg cartons. You may need to cut some cartons in half or into smaller sections to completely fill the tray.

 5 Take the egg cartons from the tray and paint them. White paint works well because it will show off the items in the display case.

 6 Paint the cardboard tray in a bright color.

7 When all the paint has dried, cover the inside of the tray with glue. Put the egg cartons back into the tray and press them onto the glue.

 8 Once the glue has dried your display case is ready. Put the rocks you find into the case. You can also buy rocks for your collection from rock, craft, and hobby stores.

Minerals, Gemstones, and Crystals

Rocks are made from solid substances called **minerals**. Some types of rock are made from just one kind of mineral. Others are a mixture of different minerals.

Granite is a type of igneous rock. It is made from minerals called feldspar, quartz, mica, and usually hornblende.

granite rock

Crystals

Minerals sometimes grow in shapes called **crystals**. A crystal has straight edges and smooth sides, called faces. Salt is a type of mineral that forms in crystals. If you look at a grain of salt through a **microscope**, you can see its crystal shape.

straight edges

a salt crystal

smooth faces

Some minerals are so beautiful they are used to make jewelry. Diamonds, rubies, and emeralds are all minerals. Pieces of these minerals are removed from rocks. They are cut into shapes and polished. Then they are known as gemstones.

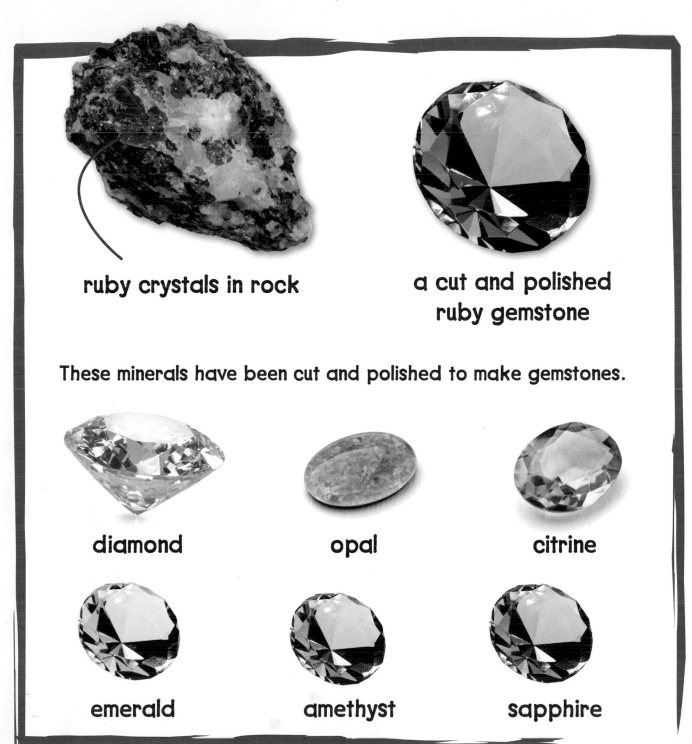

ruby crystals in rock

a cut and polished ruby gemstone

These minerals have been cut and polished to make gemstones.

diamond

opal

citrine

emerald

amethyst

sapphire

...ke Your Own ...stals

This project is also a science experiment, so you'll have to be extra careful with the ingredients. You'll get to see crystals form and use the shapes for holiday decorations!

You will need:

- Pipe cleaners
- Two pairs of rubber dishwashing gloves
- A clean, empty glass jar for each shape
- A measuring cup
- Cold water
- A tablespoon

- Borax crystals (available in the laundry aisle at the supermarket)
- Food coloring
- Pencils or chopsticks
- Boiling water
- An adult to boil and pour the water and handle the borax
- String

Get Crafty:

 1 Bend the pipe cleaners into shapes of your choice.

 2 Tie a piece of string to each shape.

3 Using cold water, measure how many cups of water each jar will hold.

4 Ask an adult to fill each jar with boiling water and add borax to each jar. For every cup of water, the adult should add 3 tablespoons of borax. So, if a jar holds two cups of water, add 6 tablespoons of borax.

5 Ask an adult to stir the boiling water and borax until all the borax has dissolved and the water looks clear.

6 If you want colored shapes, ask an adult to add two or three drops of food coloring to the water and stir.

7 Tie each pipe cleaner shape to a pencil or chopstick.

8 Finally, ask an adult to dangle one shape into each jar. The pencil should rest over the opening of the jar so the shape hangs in the water. The shape should not touch the bottom of the jar.

9 Leave the jars overnight. The next day, crystals will have formed on the pipe cleaner shapes! Have an adult help you remove the shapes from the water and allow them to dry. Be sure both of you are wearing gloves when you handle the wet crystals.

Fossils

Sometimes, scientists and rock collectors find fossils in rocks. Fossils are the rocky remains of ancient animals and plants.

When an ancient animal died, the soft parts of its body rotted away. Over many years, layers of sediment covered the animal's bones.

In time, the bones crumbled away, and sediment filled the spaces left by the bones. More and more layers of sediment settled above. The layers got heavier and heavier and pressed together to make rock.

After millions of years, fossils, or rock copies of the animal's bones, formed.

Fossil Finds

Fossils have been found of birds, fish, insects, plants, dinosaurs, and even dinosaur droppings!

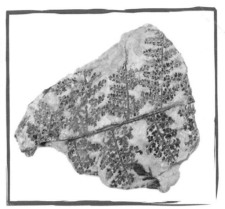

a turtle fossil   a fish fossil   fossilized plant leaves

a fossilized *Tyrannosaurus rex*

Make a Fossil

It's possible to make your own rocky fossils. It won't take millions of years for these fossils to form, however, just about 30 minutes!

You will need:

- Leaves, seashells, or any object that you want to fossilize
- Modeling clay
- Cooking oil
- A strip of cardboard about 1 inch (2.5 cm) wide
- A paper clip
- Plaster of Paris
- A bowl
- Water
- A spoon for mixing

Get Crafty:

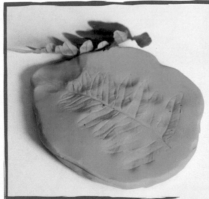

 1 Using your hands, roll out a lump of modeling clay so it is flat and smooth.

 2 Press a seashell or leaf into the clay, then remove.

 3 Rub a little cooking oil into the shape in the clay with your fingers.

4 Using the cardboard strip and paper clip, make a little collar, or wall, around the shape.

5 Put some plaster of Paris into the bowl, add some water, and start stirring. The mixture should be the thickness of pancake batter with no lumps. Keep adding plaster or water until the mix is right.

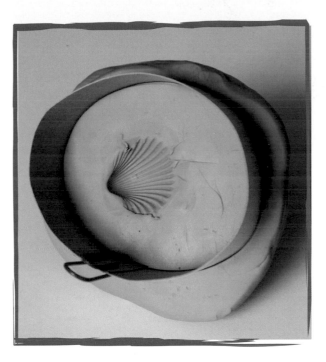

6 Spoon or pour the mix into the shape in the modeling clay and then fill the cardboard collar with plaster of Paris.

7 The plaster should set hard in about 30 minutes. Gently touch the plaster to find out if it is dry and hard. If it still feels soft, leave it for another 10 minutes and then try again.

8 When the plaster is hard and dry, gently remove the modeling clay from around the model. You will have a fossil of the object you pressed into the modeling clay!

Glossary

crust (KRUST)
The outer layer of Earth that is made of rock.

crystal (KRIS-tul)
A solid mineral that has formed in nature with a shape that has straight edges and smooth faces.

fossil (FO-sul)
An imprint of an animal or plant's remains that has formed in rock over millions of years.

igneous rock (IG-nee-us ROK)
Rock made from magma or lava that has cooled and become hard.

lava (LAH-vuh)
Magma that has escaped from underground out of a volcano.

magma (MAG-muh)
Underground rock that has become so hot it melts.

metamorphic rock
(meh-tuh-MOR-fik ROK)
Rock that has changed from one type to another because it has been pressed down upon by other rocks and heated underground.

microscope (MY-kruh-skohp)
A piece of equipment that allows a person to see a large view of an object that is too small to see with his or her eyes.

mineral (MIN-rul)
A solid substance made in nature. Rocks are made from minerals.

sculpture (SKULP-cher)
A model made from a material such as rock or wood.

sediment (SEH-deh-ment)
Tiny pieces of rock that have been worn away from bigger rocks by forces such as waves or wind.

sedimentary rock
(seh-deh-MEN-teh-ree ROK)
Rock made from many layers of sediment that have been pressed so hard they join together and become solid.

volcano (vol-KAY-noh)
A hole in the Earth's crust through which magma, or lava, escapes. Over time, a mountain of rock made from cooled lava may build up around the hole.

Websites

Due to the changing nature of Internet links, PowerKids Press has developed an online list of websites related to the subject of this book. This site is updated regularly. Please use this link to access the list:
www.powerkidslinks.com/gco/rock/

Read More

Bailey, Jacqui. *The Rock Factory: The Story About the Rock Cycle.* North Mankato, MN: Picture Window Books, 2006.

Hoffman, Stephen M. *Rock Study: A Guide to Looking at Rocks.* Rock It!. New York: PowerKids Press, 2011.

Zoehfeld, Kathleen Weidner. *Rocks and Minerals.* Des Moines, IA: National Geographic Children's Books, 2013.

Index

A
amethysts, 23

C
citrine gemstones, 23
cliffs, 10
craft projects:
    make a fossil, 28–29
    make crystals, 24–25
    pebble pictures, 16–17
    rock display case, 20–21
    rock sculptures, 8–9
    sand art paperweights,
        12–13
crust, 4, 6–7
crystals, 22–25

D
diamonds, 23
dinosaurs, 26–27
dirt, 11

E
Earth, 4, 6–7
emeralds, 5, 23

F
feldspar, 22
fossils, 26–29

G
gemstones, 23
gneiss, 18
granite, 22

H
hornblende, 22

I
igneous rocks, 5–7, 18, 22

L
lava, 7
limestone, 15

M
magma, 6–7
metal, 6
metamorphic rocks, 5–6, 18–19
mica, 22
minerals, 22–23

O
obsidian rock, 7
opals, 23

Q
quartz, 22

R
rain, 10, 15
rock collectors, 5, 18–19, 26
rubies, 23

S
salt, 22
sand, 11–13
sapphires, 23
sedimentary rocks, 5–6, 10,
    14–15, 18

V
volcanoes, 6–7

W
waves, 10
wind, 10